Module 6: Research & Online Sources

Introduction

In higher education, you need to be able to research other people's ideas and gather resources in order to support your arguments in seminars, presentations and written assignments. Many students find research particularly difficult, as they may be unclear about required academic conventions, or may have difficulty finding appropriate academic sources.

This module will take you through tasks that will clarify the importance of research in academic study, guide you through the key steps in the research process and help you find and evaluate a variety of academic sources, from online articles to books in the library.

At the end of this module, you will feel more confident about undertaking your own research on a university course.

Contents

1 Why research?

At the end of this unit, you will:

- recognise how research can develop your understanding of a topic
- understand the need to refer to sources in your academic work
- be aware of different conventions and attitudes to research in different cultures

Task 1 Why research?

You may already have a lot of general knowledge on many topics. However, in higher education, you will need to research other facts and ideas in order to develop your understanding further. This deeper knowledge will also help you support your arguments in your essays and assignments.

1.1 **Imagine you are going to write an essay on obesity. Work in groups to discuss what you already know about obesity and answer the questions.**

    a.   What is obesity?

    _____

    _____

    b.   How serious a problem do you think it is?

    _____

    _____

    c.   What causes obesity?

    _____

    _____

    d.   What impact does it have on individuals and society?

    _____

    _____

    e.   What can be done to address the problem?

    _____

    _____

1.2 **Discuss the questions with the class.**

    a.   How much did you know about obesity before your discussion?

    b.   What extra information or ideas would you need to know to write an essay on obesity?

    c.   What sources of information could help you write this essay?

Task 2 Supporting evidence and arguments

2.1   Read the extract from an essay and answer the questions. Underline the answers in the essay.

    a.   How serious is the problem of obesity?

    b.   What are its main causes?

    c.   What can governments do to combat obesity?

    d.   Why are these steps effective?

To what extent should governments regulate the eating habits of individuals in order to combat obesity?

by Andrew Student

One of the most pressing problems facing the developed world today is that of obesity. In recent years, there has been a dramatic rise in the number of obese people. This has been accompanied by an associated increase in health problems such as diabetes, heart disease and stroke. It is essential that governments take action and that they target the root causes of this problem, rather than just its symptoms. Promoting healthy eating in school will be key in combating obesity.

Obesity is defined as having too much body fat. It is generally caused by poor eating habits, most especially the overconsumption of fast food, salt and sugar.

A healthy diet is of utmost importance to all age groups, but especially children and teenagers. Governments should, therefore, engage in promotional campaigns in schools to target young people and teach them about the advantages of a well-balanced diet. School lessons could explain the advantage of eating a variety of different foods, including plenty of fruit and vegetables, some protein, some dairy foods, and only a very small amount of food that is high in fat and sugar.

Governments can also require that the food offered in schools meets minimum health standards and they can eliminate the sale and marketing of unhealthy food. Too many school cafeterias currently sell junk food to young people. If this situation is allowed to continue, young people's obesity rates will not decline.

2.2 **Work in groups to discuss the questions and write notes.**

    a.   What new information have you learned about obesity?

    b.   Has the writer shown a good knowledge of the topic?

    c.   Do you agree with the definition of obesity?

    d.   How convincing is the argument in this essay?

2.3 **Look again at the essay in Task 2.1. Underline the parts of the essay where you could add supporting points and evidence to strengthen it. Compare your answers with a partner's.**

2.4 **There are different types of supporting evidence you can use, depending on the subject area, the type of assignment and the argument you want to support. Work with a partner to answer the questions.**

    a.   What types of supporting evidence can you think of? Add to the list.

- factual information
- statistics
-
-
-
-
-

    b.   For each section of the essay you underlined in Task 2.3, discuss how you would support the argument.

> **Example**
>
> In recent years, there has been a dramatic rise in the number of obese people.
> *Add statistics indicating the increase in numbers over time.*

Task 3 Academic conventions for research

Students at UK universities are expected to understand the importance of researching sources to support their arguments and then to clearly make reference to these sources in assignments. This can involve extra work, but the benefits outweigh any drawbacks. The more you have to put into your studies the more you will get out of them. Some international students are used to different conventions and find that they need to change their approach.

3.1 **The comments below were made by four international students at British universities. Read about their experiences and discuss the questions with a partner.**

a. Have you had similar experiences?

b. What are the main differences between university writing in the UK and in these students' countries?

c. How do the international students feel about these differences?

d. What advice would you give them?

'In my country, we don't do much writing at undergraduate level. We go to lectures, take notes and learn the information. At the end of the year, we have an exam, but it's spoken. In England, you have to do so many essays. At first I found it strange, but now I like it as the essays make me think about the topics we are studying and I can use the essays to help me revise for exams.'

Kris

Bo

'I am a Science student, and the way we write our reports is so different to how people do it here in the UK. One thing is the length. In the UK, writers add a lot of stuff, which is totally irrelevant and boring. The beginnings and the ends of the reports are full of quotations from other people's research. In my country, we talk about the problem, the methodology and the solution. There is no point talking about other people's work. It's in the library and a good student knows it already. It is boring to mention it again.'

'I've written essays before, but at school my tutors didn't ask me to do a lot of extra reading on my own before I started. I thought that good students had enough ideas from attending class to begin writing. I didn't spend too much time reading, for fear I wouldn't have enough time to write the essay properly. If I needed something extra, I could get a bit of information quickly and easily from the internet.'

Edward

Phan

'In my country, we are taught not to steal other people's ideas or writing. So when we do university writing, we write a list of all the books we have used in a bibliography. We don't give a reference in the text of our essay. It's enough to mention the books in our bibliographies. Also, if the idea is well known or if it comes from a lecture, we don't mention it in a bibliography because the tutors and students know where the idea is from. At first, I kept forgetting this type of thing in my bibliographies, but now I am beginning to change.'

1

Reflect

Think about the academic conventions for research that you are used to. Write a summary of the main differences between university writing in the UK and in your country.

what I'm used to	what is expected of me now

2   The research process

At the end of this unit, you will:

- be able to prepare appropriate research questions
- identify different types of research (primary, secondary)
- be aware of the range of sources of information available and their usefulness
- be able to document your research by keeping a detailed list of sources

Task 1 Sources of information

1.1   Look at the list of sources of information in the table and discuss their strengths and weaknesses. Refer to your own experience of using these sources. Make notes in the table.

You should consider:

a.   authority

b.   ease of access

c.   reliability

d.   amount of and type of information

e.   relevance

f.   date published

What else might you consider?

- _____
- _____
- _____

source	strengths	weaknesses
textbooks		
websites		
government (or other official) documents		
academic journal articles		
dictionaries & encyclopedias		
newspaper or magazine articles		
eTextbooks		

Task 2 Evaluating sources of information

2.1 Read the texts (a–f) and consider the type of publication they come from (refer to the list in Task 1). Complete the table.

	text a	text b	text c	text d	text e	text f
type of text						
reliability and authority						
currency (up to date)						
usefulness (If so, for what?)						
language – (in)formal, (im)personal						

a.

Britain's obesity crisis is so serious that hospitals are buying specialist equipment to keep bodies cool because they are too large to fit into mortuary fridges. Hospitals are also having to widen corridors, buy reinforced beds and lifting equipment in order to cope with the growing numbers of obese patients coming though their doors. Figures obtained by *The Telegraph* show that hospitals have spent at least £5.5 million over the past three years to adapt in order to allow them to treat larger patients. Experts now warn the cost of treating overweight and obese patients could rise to at least £10 million a year as the nation's waistlines continue expanding. A quarter of adults in the UK are estimated to be obese and the number is expected to grow to account for more than half of the population in the next 30 years. Already, hospitals are having to buy specialist beds, wheelchairs, commodes and crutches for obese patients to help them deal with the crisis, a Freedom of Information request has revealed. Yeovil District Hospital NHS Trust spent £15,000 on a bariatric body cooling system, which is used to keep the bodies of obese patients cool, when they do not fit in standard-size mortuary fridges. The Queen Elizabeth Hospital in Kings Lynn spent £30,000 on a bariatric body store fridge for obese patients in 2013 and, the year after, spent £20,000 to strengthen an operating theatre floor. Doncaster and Bassetlaw NHS Trust spent £80,000 widening corridors to accommodate obese patients, while Milton Keynes Hospital spent £65 a day hiring a bed capable of holding a patient weighing almost half a ton (400 kg).

Source: http://www.telegraph.co.uk/news/health/news/10901487/Hospitals-buy-special-fridges-to-store-overweight-bodies-as-obesity-crisis-escalates.html

b.

The many chronic and acute health disorders associated with excess bodyweight burden a society not only by negatively affecting the health-related quality of life (Muennig et al., 2006) of its people, but also by incurring substantial costs to the individuals affected and to society, notably from increased health care costs and lost productivity. The medical costs of obesity represent the monetary value of health care resources devoted to managing obesity-related disorders, including the costs incurred by excess use of ambulatory care, hospitalisation, drugs, radiological or laboratory tests, and long-term care (including nursing homes). In a systematic review of the direct health care costs of obesity, Withrow et al. (2011) estimated that obesity accounted for up to 2.8% of health care expenditure, noting that the studies were generally very conservative, such that the actual amount was likely to be higher. On the basis of the most recent US data, Finkelstein et al. (2009) reported that, compared with normal–weight individuals, obese patients incur 46% increased inpatient costs, 27% more physician visits and outpatient costs, and 80% increased spending on prescription drugs. The annual extra medical costs of obesity in the USA were estimated as $75 billion in 2003 and accounted for 4–7% of total health care expenditure.

Source: Adapted from: http://www.thelancet.com/pdfs/journals/lancet/PIIS0140-6736%2811%2960814-3.pdf

c.

The relationship between food prices and obesity can be shown in terms of the cost of a Big Mac (the most popular McDonald's burger) priced in terms of average wages: countries with the lowest-cost Big Macs have the highest male obesity levels. This association is not so strong for female obesity levels for reasons that are not clear. Aggressive promotional marketing provides consumers with messages about what they should be eating, and frequently they may not support the recommended diets for health. Some 70% of the food advertising on children's TV is for food containing high levels of fat and/or sugars. A ten-country survey found the extent of such advertising is associated with levels of overweight children.

Source: https://www.gov.uk/government/uploads/system/uploads/attachment_data/file/295683/07-926A1-obesity-international.pdf

d.

Overweight and obesity are defined as abnormal or excessive fat accumulation that may impair health. Body mass index (BMI) is a simple index of weight-for-height that is commonly used to classify overweight and obesity in adults. It is defined as a person's weight in kilograms divided by the square of a person's height in meters (kg/m^2). The WHO definition is:

- a BMI greater than or equal to 25 is overweight
- a BMI greater than or equal to 30 is obesity

BMI provides the most useful population-level measure of overweight and obesity levels, as it is the same for both sexes and for all ages of adults. However, it should be considered a rough guide because it may not correspond to the same degree of fatness in different individuals.

Source: http://www.who.int/mediacentre/factsheets/fs311/en/

e.

malnutrition (n) a lack of proper nutrition, caused by not having enough to eat, not eating enough of the right things, or being unable to use the food that one does eat

Source: Adapted from http://www.oxforddictionaries.com/definition/english/malnutrition

f.

The UK government, especially through its four departments of health and also through other agencies, such as local councils, has acted to address the wider determinants of health and to engage with communities and individuals in an attempt to ensure a better understanding of good health and its link to a nutritious and balanced diet and to an increase in physical activity. Many primary care trusts in England, for example, are producing nutritional and activity initiatives targeted at local communities and individuals at high risk of becoming obese. A large amount of funding, about £30 million, was made available at the end of 2008 to support local authorities in creating more parks and cycle paths to make it easier for residents to keep fit.

Source: *The Obesity Epidemic and its Management* (2010) Maguire, Terry; Haslam, David http://lib.myilibrary.com.idpproxy.reading.

2

Task 3 Preparing research questions

Research questions are questions you identify in order to guide your research. You may need to add to this list of questions as your research progresses.

3.1 Choose one of the essay titles (a–f). Make a list of research questions.

a. Modern lifestyles need to change as technology can no longer keep up with the demands man is placing on the planet. Discuss.

b. What can be done to ensure that the world's cities are liveable for future generations?

c. To what extent has the internet affected the lives of students?

d. Social media has had a positive impact on reducing crime levels in cities. Discuss.

e. Globalisation is having a negative effect on the environment. Discuss.

f. Give an example of a smart material and explain its properties and applications.

3.2 In Unit 1, Task 2 you looked at an essay entitled: *To what extent should governments regulate the eating habits of individuals in order to combat obesity?* **Make a list of six research questions for this title.**

a. _Which eating habits cause obesity?_

b. _____

c. _____

d. _____

e. _____

f. _____

Task 4 Researching

4.1 **Before you start your research, work with a partner to answer the questions.**

    a.   Why do you need to make notes as you research?

    b.   What information should you include in your notes?

    c.   How much information should you write?

    d.   Why do you need to record bibliographical details with your notes?

4.2 **Find two sources which help to answer one of the research questions you wrote in Task 3.2. Remember to think about the reliability and authority of your sources.**

As you review your two sources, write brief notes and keep a record of the bibliographical details in the relevant tables.

You will learn more about writing bibliographies and note-taking in the *Referencing & Avoiding Plagiarism* module of the TASK series.

books					
author's family name and initial(s)	date of publication	title	edition	place of publication	publisher

websites				
author's family name and initial(s)	when last updated	title	date you accessed site	web address

Task 5 Types of research

There are two main types of research: primary research and secondary research.

5.1 Read the statements and decide whether they relate to primary research (P) or secondary research (S).

a.   The researcher gathers original data by conducting experiments.   _P_

b.   The researcher gathers existing data that has already been produced.   ___

c.   The researcher gathers data from members of the public, who take part in interviews
     or experiments.   ___

d.   The researcher gathers data already published, such as reports in newspapers.   ___

e.   The researcher designs questionnaires and/or surveys.   ___

5.2 Look again at the essay titles in Task 3.1. Work with a partner to discuss which of the titles are likely to require data gathered through primary research and which are likely to require data gathered through secondary research.

primary research	secondary research

5.3 What sort of primary and secondary research could you do to answer the following research question? How could you gather data?

> To what extent has the internet affected the lives of students?

_____

_____

_____

_____

Reflect

In Task 2.1, you evaluated several sources of information. Look again at the sources you identified as useful and reflect on how they could help you write the essay: *To what extent should governments regulate the eating habits of individuals in order to combat obesity?*

3 Finding and evaluating sources online

At the end of this unit, you will be able to:

- understand various types of online sources and their purpose
- evaluate the quality and reliability of online sources
- select online sources for your use in research

Many students like to use the internet to do research for their academic work because it is a rich and easily accessible source of information. As you saw in Unit 2, there are both strengths and weaknesses associated with the use of webpages as sources of information.

Task 1 Using the internet for academic research

1.1 **Work in groups. Spend five minutes discussing the internet and academic research, then answer the questions.**

a. How much experience have you had of using the internet to do academic research in the past?

_____

_____

b. Are there any websites or online sources that you have found especially useful?

_____

_____

c. Explain how you found these sources and why you thought they were useful.

_____

_____

How much information is available online? Counting the total number of webpages in existence is almost impossible, but estimates put the number in the billions. The results of any web search will often provide a huge number of results.

1.2 **In a recent online search for 'world population', how many results do you think were provided by the search engine? Circle the correct answer.**

a. 110,000,000

b. 1,010,000

c. 100,000

3

Task 2 Searching the web

2.1 Because of the size of the internet, you need to be selective in choosing what you use as a source. Read the paragraph about doing online searches and complete the sentences using some of the words from the box.

Scholar	~~internet search engines~~	databases	subjects
academic	keywords	journal	statistics

Nowadays, most people use _internet search engines_ to find information online. These are software systems that search all over the World Wide Web, and some of the most well-known include *Google*, *Bing* and *Ask*. They are quick and easy to use: you enter your search terms or ^a _____ and receive a list of results to choose from. However, they also have limitations, when used for ^b _____ research and students are often advised to consider using alternatives such as Google ^c _____, or library ^d _____, which can be especially valuable in finding ^e _____ articles and resources for particular academic ^f _____.

When searching for sources online, it is important to carefully select your search terms, using keywords, to make your research faster and more efficient.

2.2 Work with a partner to discuss the questions.

a. What keywords will help you search for information relevant to this research question: *What effect does fast-food advertising have on children?*

_____

_____

b. How can the search operators *and*, *or* and *not* be used to narrow or widen your search?

_____

_____

c. How can placing a phrase between quotation marks (e.g., 'fast-food advertising') help your search results?

_____

_____

Task 3 Evaluating webpages

Almost anyone can put information on the internet, so it is essential to critically evaluate any website before you use it as a source.

3.1 Look at three different sections of a webpage and answer the questions.

    a.   Who is responsible for producing the material on this page? _____

    b.   What expertise does the writer/publisher have? _____

    c.   Does the writer demonstrate any bias? _____

    d.   Are the statistical data on this page primary or secondary? _____

    e.   When was the webpage published and/or updated? _____

    f.   What does *gov* mean in the web address? _____

1.

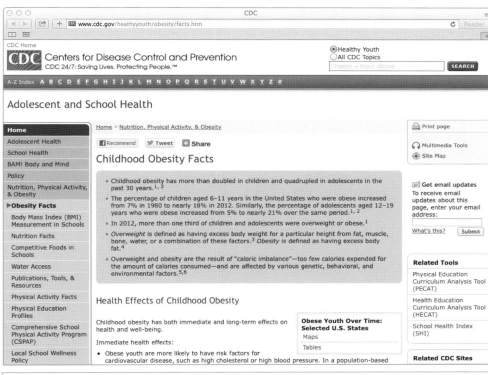

2.

    References

    1. Ogden CL, Carroll MD, Kit BK, Flegal KM. Prevalence of childhood and adult obesity in the United States, 2011-2012. *Journal of the American Medical Association* 2014;311(8):806-814.

    2. National Center for Health Statistics. Health, United States, 2011: With Special Features on Socioeconomic Status and Health. Hyattsville, MD; U.S. Department of Health and Human Services; 2012.

    3. National Institutes of Health, National Heart, Lung, and Blood Institute. Disease and Conditions Index: What Are Overweight and Obesity? Bethesda, MD: National Institutes of Health; 2010.

3.

    Print   Multimedia   Site Map

    File Formats Help:

    Page last reviewed: December 11, 2014
    Page last updated: December 11, 2014

    How do I view different file formats (PDF, DOC, PPT, MPEG) on this site? »

    Content source: National Center for HIV/AIDS, Viral Hepatitis, STD, and TB Prevention, Division of Adolescent and School Health and National Center for Chronic Disease Prevention and Health Promotion, Division of Population Health

    Home   A-Z Index   Policies   Using this Site   Link to Us   Contact CDC

    Centers for Disease Control and Prevention   1600 Clifton Road Atlanta, GA 30329-4027, USA
    800-CDC-INFO (800-232-4636) TTY: (888) 232-6348 - Contact CDC-INFO

    USA.gov
    Government Made Easy

The URL (uniform resource locator) is the address of a webpage, and it can give you information about a website, such as the type of author/organisation who created it, or the country where the website is registered.

3.2 **Match the domain name extensions (a–f) with the information they reveal (1–6).**

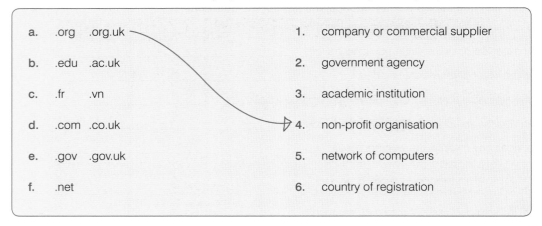

a. .org   .org.uk

b. .edu   .ac.uk

c. .fr   .vn

d. .com .co.uk

e. .gov   .gov.uk

f. .net

1. company or commercial supplier

2. government agency

3. academic institution

4. non-profit organisation

5. network of computers

6. country of registration

3.3 **After the domain name, many websites have subdirectory or file name information that can tell you more about the website.**

a. Work with a partner to discuss the following URLs and decide what kind of websites they are.

   1. http://www.reading.ac.uk/library
   2. https://www.goodreads.com/blog/
   3. http://www.nutrition.org.uk/publications
   4. http://en.wikipedia.org/wiki/List_of_best-selling_books

b. What are *blogs* and *wikis*? What are the possible disadvantages of using them for academic research?

_____

_____

_____

_____

_____

3.4 Work with a partner to discuss what you should do if the URL does not provide any clues about the page. How would you find out more about the publisher of the webpage below?

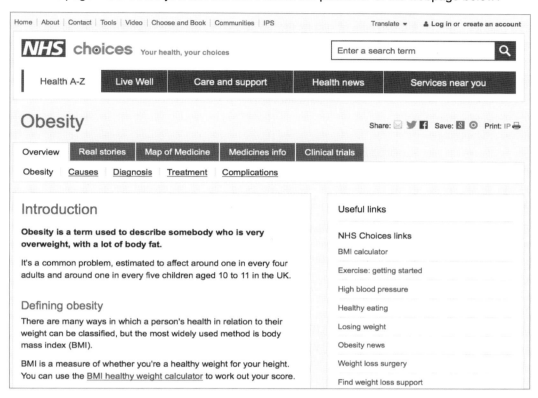

3

Task 4 Practising website evaluation

4.1 Work with a partner. Look at the two sets of results for the search terms 'government regulation healthy eating' and answer the questions for each result.

    a. Did the result come from a search on *Google* or *Google Scholar*?

    b. What can you tell about the webpage?

    c. Does the page seem relevant to the search terms above?

    d. How academic is the page?

    e. Is the page up to date?

    f. Would you click on the page to read more? Why/Why not?

The politics of obesity: seven steps to government action
R Kersh, J Morone - Health Affairs, 2002 - Health Affairs
Abstract Concern is rapidly growing about **obesity** rates in the United States. This paper analyses the **political** consequences. Despite myths about individualism and self-reliance, the US **government** has a long tradition of regulating ostensibly private behaviour. We draw ...
Cited by 112   Related articles   All 6 versions   Cite   Save

---

'Put pictures of fat people on junk food to show ... - Daily Mail
www.dailymail.co.uk/.../The-food-industry-regulated-like-tobacc...   Daily Mail ▾
May 19, 2014 - Food packaging should include pictures of the damage obesity can cause health, similar to those on cigarette packets, campaigners said today.

4.2 In Unit 4, you will learn more about library databases, which you can also search online, and which you can use to find reliable and authoritative sources.

Look at the library database search result for 'government regulation healthy eating' and answer questions b–f in Task 4.1. Compare your answers with a partner's.

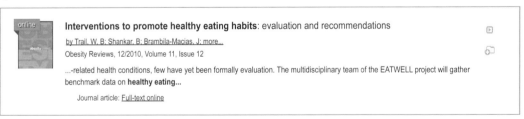

Reflect

What have you learned about evaluating online sources? Complete the Evaluation checklist and then apply it to two online sources you have already found for an essay.

Evaluation checklist

	source 1	source 2
	URL:	URL:
relevance		
Is the website directly relevant to your topic?		
authority		
Who produced the website?		
What level of expertise do they have?		
reliability		
Does it provide facts or opinions?		
currency		

4 Understanding and using academic books and journals

At the end of this unit, you will:

- understand the importance of the peer review process and its impact on academic journals
- know how to search library databases for academic books and journals
- evaluate the relevance and usefulness of academic books and journals in your research

Task 1 Understanding academic journals

As you have seen in previous units, academic journals are a reliable source of information and can be found online in university libraries.

Academic journals are publications which present new research, and critique and review existing research. They are a way for researchers and scholars to share their research with the academic community. Most academic disciplines have their own journals made up of articles written for experts or researchers in that discipline. Academic journals are usually published periodically, for example, monthly or quarterly. You can learn about specific areas of your topic in great detail.

1.1 **Below are three academic journals. Which articles do you think will be published in each of the journals? Write 1, 2 or 3 in the box.**

1. **British Journal of Psychology**	2. *Cambridge Journal of Economics*	3. New Journal of Physics

a.   *Governance, regulation and financial market instability: The implications for policy.*   __2__

b.   *Apparent correction to the speed of light in a gravitational potential.*   ____

c.   *Why is intelligence associated with stability of happiness?*   ____

d.   *Limited liability, shareholder rights and the problem of corporate irresponsibility.*   ____

e.   *Focus on correlation effects in radiation fields.*   ____

f.   *When does anxiety help or hinder test performance? The role of working memory capacity.*   ____

Academic journals are especially useful for your research as they provide reliable information. This is because they are peer reviewed.

1.2 **Which of the definitions define *peer review*? Circle the correct answer.**

a.   The evaluation of scientific, academic or professional work by journal publishers.

b.   The evaluation of scientific, academic or professional work by others working in the same field.

c.   A report on the usefulness of a piece of written work by students.

1.3 **Complete the paragraph using some of the words in the box.**

scholarship	written	research	valid	judge
reliable	~~evaluated~~	scholars	biased	objective

All articles submitted to a journal are *evaluated* by several respected ᵃ_____ in the same discipline. They ᵇ_____ whether the article is ᶜ_____, ᵈ_____ and ᵉ_____ and should be published. Peer review ensures high quality ᶠ_____ in a discipline. This means that journal articles are valuable for your academic ᵍ_____.

Task 2 Searching library databases for journals

In Unit 2, you made list of questions which you need to research to write the essay entitled: *To what extent should governments regulate the eating habits of individuals in order to combat obesity?*

You are now going to look at the following research question: *What eating habits cause obesity?*

If you are a university student, you could research answers to this question using your online university library database. There are two main ways to search your online university library database.

1.   Search by subject
Sometimes it is easy to identify which subject your research relates to. When you click on the subject, your university library database will take you to a facility to search for a topic relating to that particular subject. This means your search results will be narrowed down and irrelevant results are less likely to appear.

2.1   Work with a partner to answer the questions.

a.   Look at the alphabetical list of subjects and decide which subject relates to the essay question: *What eating habits cause obesity?*

Accounting
Business
Chemistry
Economics
Food and Nutritional Sciences
Geography and Environmental Science
Law
Management, Accounting and Informatics
Politics and International Relations
Real Estate and Planning

b.   It is important to use keywords to carry out your search. Which of the keyword options should you use to research your question? Circle the correct answer.

1.   obesity

2.   eating habits

3.   What eating habits cause obesity?

4.   eating and obesity

c.   Explain your choice and discuss it with a partner.

_____

_____

_____

2. Search by keywords

As you saw in Unit 3, Task 2, it is important to carefully select your search terms when using online sources. The same applies when you use a university library database. For example, search operators *and*, *or* and *not* can be used to narrow or widen your searches. In Unit 4, Task 2.1, question b, the operator *and* was used to research articles about 'eating *and* obesity'. Without *and* your results may include articles about only *eating* or only *obesity*.

2.2 Look at the search results listed for 'eating and obesity'. Which of these journal titles may help you with your research? Explain your answer and discuss with a partner.

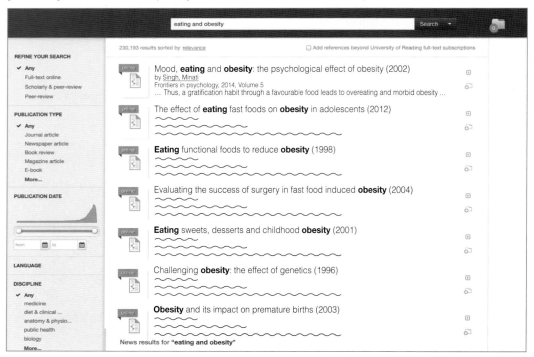

2.3 If it is difficult to identify which subject your research relates to or if your research relates to several topics, you may need to search the entire library database. Why might this be more difficult for you? Discuss with a partner.

It is important to learn the search tips of your online university library database. For example, you may be able to specify a search for keywords, authors, years or titles.

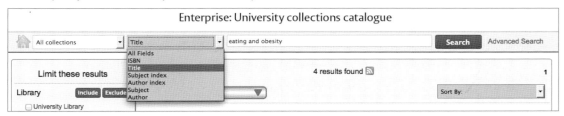

Enterprise: University collections catalogue

| All collections | Title | eating and obesity | Search | Advanced Search |

All Fields
ISBN
Title
Subject index
Author index
Subject
Author

Limit these results   4 results found   1

Library   Include Exclude   Sort By:

☐ University Library

2.4 This student did not make very effective notes. How could he search the university library database to find the four sources again?

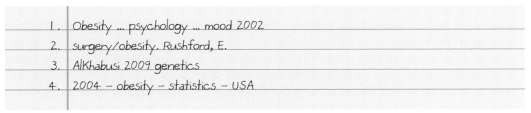

1. Obesity ... psychology ... mood 2002
2. surgery/obesity. Rushford, E.
3. AlKhabusi 2009 genetics
4. 2004 – obesity – statistics – USA

4

Task 3 Using abstracts

Abstracts are usually found at the beginning of journal articles. They provide a summary of the article. Abstracts usually include:

- conclusion
- thesis statement or aim
- results or findings
- context of the study
- method of the research
- background

3.1 **Identify which sentence (a–f) in the abstract provides the information usually found in an abstract listed above.**

a. _background_

b. _____

c. _____

d. _____

e. _____

f. _____

Abstract

[a] A causal relationship between hunger and obesity in the US has previously been suggested. Two recent studies have found evidence to suggest an association between obesity and food insecurity among adult women, and a third study suggests an association between being underweight and food insecurity among men. [b] The purpose of the current study is to investigate the association between obesity in an adult population and concern about enough food [c] in two Chinese cities. [d] A cross-sectional analysis was conducted using data from the Behavioural Risk Factor Surveillance System (2002). [e] An 8.0% prevalence of concern about enough food was found in Beijing, and an 11.8% prevalence was found in Ningbo, and this concern was positively associated with morbid obesity. [f] A very strong apparent relationship was identified between concern about enough food and obesity in these two Chinese cities.

Source: Adapted from http://www.sciencedirect.com/science/article/pii/S009174350300238X

3.2 **Work with a partner to discuss and make notes about how you can use abstracts to help your research.**

_____

_____

_____

_____

_____

Task 4 Academic books

Your tutor may give you a reading list which is likely to include academic book titles. You may also find that reference material, such as encyclopedias or dictionaries, is helpful.

4.1 The academic books found in a university library are reliable, valid and objective. Why do you think this is? Discuss with a partner.

4.2 Books found in a university library have been selected because they contain reliable information, and are written by experts and academics. Several different people decide which books should be available in a university library. From the list below, tick the people who you think are involved in these decisions.

a. tutors ☐

b. lecturers ☐

c. publishers ☐

d. university librarians ☐

e. bookshop managers ☐

f. the government ☐

g. authors ☐

4.3 Read the ten statements (a–j) and decide which type(s) of source (1–3) each one refers to (more than one type is possible).

1. academic books
2. academic journals
3. online sources

a. It is easy to identify who the author is. _____

b. The author's writing has been judged reliable and valid for publication. _____

c. It is possible to find this type of source suitable for your level, for example, less or more complex. _____

d. There may not be editors or reviewers who will check facts and figures. _____

e. Information for a bibliography, such as publisher, author, editor and date of publication, is always clearly listed. _____

f. It is easy to identify who produced statistics, graphs and tables in this type of source. _____

g. You can read through the table of contents to see whether your topic is discussed in enough detail. _____

h. It may not be possible to see the academic qualifications of the author. _____

i. It is not always clear when the source was published or updated. _____

j. Statistics and facts have been verified by reviewers. _____

Reflect

How has your essay on obesity been improved by the addition of your research? Think about how the skills you have used in this research could be used in subjects such as Science, Maths, Engineering, etc.

Web work

Website 1

Evaluating web sources

http://www.vtstutorials.ac.uk/detective/

Review

The Internet Detective is a guide to critically evaluating resources available on the web.

Task

Visit the site and complete the interactive tutorial.

Website 2

Primary research

https://owl.english.purdue.edu/owl/resource/559/01/

Review

A useful resource to help you conduct research using primary sources.

Task

Read through the sections to understand the nature of primary research, common issues and different types of research you can do.

Website 3

Summarising and note-taking

http://www.uefap.com/reading/readfram.htm

Review

A website with guidance and practice exercises to help you make notes and summarise academic reading texts.

Task

Click on the 'Exercises' tab and complete the exercises.

Website 4

How to read an academic article

http://faculty.washington.edu/davidgs/ReadArticle.html

Review

Learn more about how to read academic articles.

Task

Read through the advice and make notes that will help you to improve your reading skills.

Extension activities

Activity 1

Visit all of the webpages and critically evaluate how useful each one would be as a source for the research question: *Can exercise help tackle teenage obesity?*

Link between inactivity and obesity queried: http://www.bbc.co.uk/news/10545542

Physical activity and young people: http://www.who.int/dietphysicalactivity/factsheet_young_people/en/

Obesity in the UK: http://www.birmingham.ac.uk/research/activity/mds/centres/obesity/obesity-uk/index.aspx

Tackling childhood obesity: http://exercise.about.com/cs/exercisehealth/a/childobesity_2.htm

Activity 2

Visit the webpage http://scholar.google.co.uk/. Search for statistics which support the argument: *Teenage obesity is increasing.*

Critically evaluate the sources you find and consider whether they can be used for your research.

Activity 3

Reflect on the exercises you have completed in this module. What advice would you give to other students about conducting academic research? Write your top five tips.

Glossary

abstract (n) These are usually found at the beginning of journal articles. They provide a summary of the article.

academic conventions (n) The way an academic institution expects you to carry out work, such as research.

access (a site) (v) To go to a website.

authority (n) The legitimacy and validity of a source. This could involve checking who the author is and their qualifications.

biased (adj) A tendency to show favour towards or against one opinion or one group of people. A biased source does not present both sides of an argument; it is not very objective, reliable or valid.

bibliography (n) A list of references to sources cited in the text of a piece of academic writing or a book. A bibliography should consist of an alphabetical list of books, papers, journal articles and websites and is usually found at the end of the work.

currency (n) Dates to indicate when the source was written and first published, or when the content was last updated. A lot of information is time sensitive so it is important to use the most up-to-date information in your research.

data (n) Facts or information that are used to find out things or to make decisions or judgements.

database (n) An organized set of data that is stored in a computer and which can be looked at and used in various ways. For example, a library database can be used to find academic articles and resources that relate to particular academic topics.

domain name (n) This is a name that identifies a website or group of websites on the internet.

evaluate (v) To assess information in terms of its quality, relevance, objectivity and accuracy.

evidence (n) Reasons which support an idea or theory.

general knowledge (n) This is your knowledge of facts about different subjects.

journal (n) A publication that is issued at regular and stated intervals, such as every month or quarter, which contains articles and essays by different authors. Journals include magazines and newspapers as well as academic periodicals that contain more scholarly articles on specialised topics.

keyword (n) A word or phrase that you type into an online search engine to find out information about something.

objective (adj) Not influenced by personal feelings or opinions. An objective essay supports an argument with research rather than presenting the author's own opinions and ideas.

peer review (n) The process whereby an article is scrutinized and critiqued by others working in the same area before it is published. A peer-reviewed article is considered to be more reliable and credible due to this process.

primary research (n) Primary research involves gathering original data from members of the public by conducting experiments, for example, designing and carrying out surveys and questionnaires.

quotation (n) A part of a text written or spoken by one author and reproduced in a text, piece of academic writing or talk by another author. When you quote someone's words or ideas, you do not change the wording at all and should put it in inverted commas ('~') to signal that it is a quotation.

relevance (n) A close connection with the subject you are discussing or topic you are researching. When writing an essay, it is important to find sources that are relevant to your essay title.

reliability (n) The quality of the source. An academic source should be checked to ensure that it is true, up to date and credible.

research question (n) A statement or question that helps you to start gathering together ideas, notes and information in a focused way in preparation for writing an essay, report, presentation or dissertation.

scholar (n) A person who is an expert in a particular area or academic discipline, because they have studied it in detail.

search engine (n) A website comprising a large database of other websites. A search engine's 'spider' collects webpages and the search engine then allows visitors to do a keyword search to find relevant pages.

search operators (n) These are special characters and words, for example, *and*, *or* and *not*, that are used to narrow or widen your search results.

secondary research (n) Secondary research involves gathering existing data that has already been produced and published, for example, researching the internet, newspapers and company reports.

seminar (n) A small group discussion led by a tutor, lecturer or guest speaker. Students are expected to take an active part in the seminar.

source (n) Something (usually a book, articles or other text) that supplies you with information. In an academic context, sources used in essays and reports must be acknowledged.

statistics (n) A collection of information shown in numbers that can be used to explain, describe and support concepts.

supporting evidence (n) It is necessary to provide supporting evidence to strengthen your arguments in an academic essay. This support may include reference to other sources, quotations and data.

unique resource locator (URL) (n) The address of a webpage that appears in the browser.

valid (adj) An idea or argument which is based on logic and fact.

Notes

Notes

Notes

Published by
Garnet Publishing Ltd.
8 Southern Court
South Street
Reading RG1 4QS, UK

ISBN 978 1 78260 181 4

British Library Cataloguing-in-Publication Data

A catalogue record for this book is available from the British Library.

Production

Project Manager:	Clare Chandler
Editorial team:	Clare Chandler, Kate Kemp
Design & Layout:	Simon Ellway, Madeleine Maddock
Photography:	iStockphoto

Garnet Publishing and the authors of TASK would like to thank the staff and students of the International Foundation Programme at the University of Reading for their respective roles in the development of these teaching materials.

Garnet Publishing would like to thank Jane Brooks for her contribution to the First edition of the TASK series.

All website URLs provided in this publication were correct at the time of printing. If any URL does not work, please contact your tutor, who will help you find similar resources.

Printed and bound in Lebanon by International Press: interpress@int-press.com

Acknowledgements

Page 8: Text A, *Hospitals buy special fridges to store overweight bodies as obesity crisis escalates*, reproduced with kind permission of The Telegraph © Telegraph Media Group Limited 2014.

Page 9: Text B, reprinted from The Lancet, Vol. 378 Issue 9793, Y Claire Wang, Klim McPherson, Tim Marsh, Steven L Gortmaker, Martin Brown, *Health and economic burden of the projected obesity trends in the USA and the UK*, 2011 with permission from Elsevier Ltd.

Page 9: Text C, *The relationship between food prices and obesity* by the Government Office for Science, contains public sector information licensed under the Open Government Licence v3.0.

Page 9: Text D, *Obesity and overweight text*, sourced from http://www.who.int/mediacentre/factsheets/fs311/en reproduced with kind permission of the World Health Organization February 2015.

Page 9: Text E, definition of *malnutrition* from the Oxford Dictionary, reproduced with kind permission of Oxford University Press. Copyright © Oxford University Press 2015.

Page 9: Text F, Maguire, T and Haslam, D. *The Obesity Epidemic and its Management*. Pharmaceutical Press, 2010, p. 109.

Page 15: Centers for Disease Control and Prevention, *Childhood Obesity Facts* screenshot. (2014).

Page 17: NHS Choices Obesity screenshot, reproduced with kind permission of NHS Choices.

Page 18: Journal cover, from the Wiley Online Library, *Interventions to promote healthy eating habits: evaluation and recommendations* by Traill, W, B et al. Obesity reviews, 12/2010, Volume 11, Issue 12, reproduced with kind permission of the International Association for the Study of Obesity © 2010 The Authors, obesity reviews © 2010 International Association for the Study of Obesity.

Page 20: Definition of *peer review* from the Oxford Dictionary, reproduced with kind permission of Oxford University Press. Copyright © Oxford University Press 2015.

Pages 22 and 23: The screen shots and their contents are published with permission of ProQuest LLC. Further reproduction is prohibited without permission. Inquiries may be made to: ProQuest LLC, 789 E. Eisenhower Pkwy, Ann Arbor, MI 48106-1346 USA. Telephone (734) 761-4700; E-mail: info@proquest.com; Web-page: www.proquest.com

Page 24: Abstract, *Preventive Medicine* by Laraia, B. A., Siega-Riz, A. M., Evenson, K. R., Volume 38, Issue 2, February 2004, Pages 175–181, reproduced with kind permission of Elsevier.